"CRUCIFY HIM!" "Crucify him!"

"Crucify him!"

"Crucify him!"

"Crucify him!"

him!"

"Crucify him!"

"Crucify him!"

"Crucify him!" "CRUCIFY HIM!" "Crucify h

"CRUCIFY him

ify him!"

"CRUCIFY HIM!"

"Crucify him!"

"Crucify him!"

fy him!"

"CRUCIFY HIM!"

"Crucify him!"

"Crucify him!"

"Cr

"Crucify h

Crucify him!"

"Crucify him!"

"Crucify him!"

"Crucify him!"

remember man

remember

AVE MARIA PRESS
Notre Dame, Indiana 46556

man

a lenten coffee table reader
for people who seldom find
time for lenten reading

compiled and designed by
charles e. jones

photo credits

ronald brander, 3, 33, 37, 54, 55, 90, 91, 92, 93; justin soleta, 12, 49, 59, 62, 64, 76, 78, 91, 92, 93; anthony rowland, front cover, 4, 94; john lanzone, 14, back cover; william conyers, 57; michael rider, 79, 80, 88; vernon sigl, 52, 56, 70, 73; israel tourist service, 38; oeo photo, 16; religious news service, 16, 58; wide world, 16, 61, 63, 66, 67, 68, 69, 71, 72; upi, 60; unicef, 65; usda, 93; *the redeemer,* 44; *ben hur,* 43, 45, 47; *the gospel according to st. matthew,* 15, 40, 41, 42, 46, 47, 48, 49, 74.

library of congress catalog card number: 79-149591

printed in the united states of america.

ISBN: 0-87793-032-5 (cloth)
0-87793-033-3 (paperback)

contents
contents
contents
contents
contents
contents
contents
contents
contents
contents
contents
contents
contents
contents
contents
contents
contents
contents
contents
contents
contents

man remember
nber man rem
emember man
nan remember
ber man reme
member man
n remember r
r man remem
ember man re
remember ma
man rememb
nber man rem
emember man
nan remember
ber man reme
member man
n remember
r man remem
ember man re

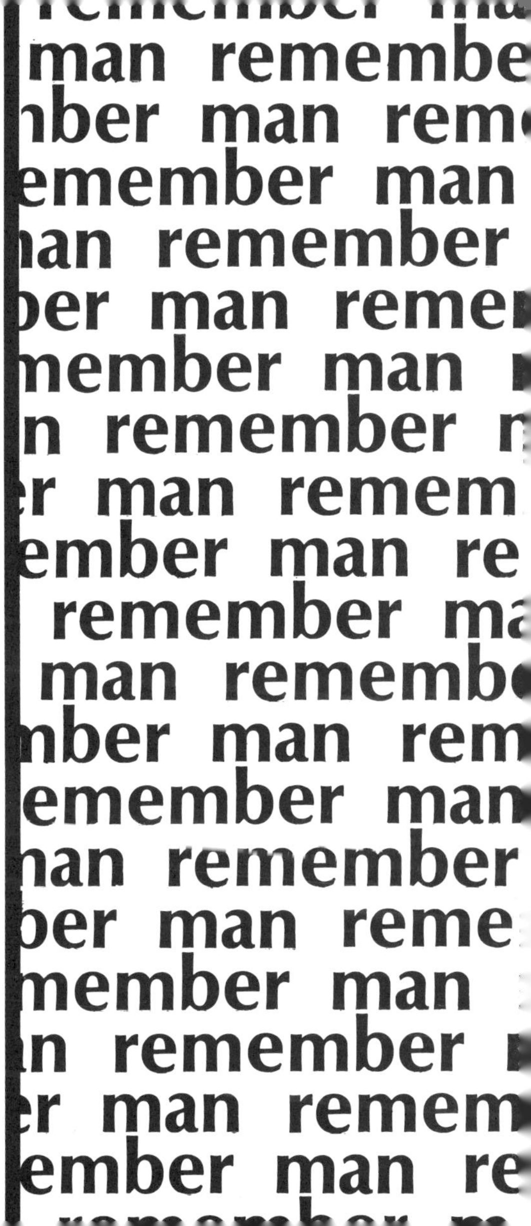

The ashes from the Easter palm
. . . bring the Lenten season on
And softly signed upon our heads
Recall those words from Scripture read,
Which if we care (and care we must)
Will fill our hearts with deep concern:

remember

man

thou art but dust
And unto dust thou shalt return.

thou art dust

One of Christianity's greatest gifts to the world is Ash Wednesday, the feast of humility. A man kneels silently while ashes are rubbed on his forehead and the priest tells him: "Remember, man that thou art dust and unto dust thou shalt return." A simple act, simple words; but they stir up deep echoes if you let them.

In a sense, it is everyman's version of a ceremony that only a few men— less than 300 in 20 centuries—have experienced. It recalls that moment in the pomp of a papal coronation procession when a humble attendant stands before the new pope and burns a handful of dry straw. One quick flash of flame and it is gone, and the attendant tells the pope: "*Sic transit gloria mundi,* thus passes the glory of the world."

Notice what is missing in both of these expressions. No mention of the soul, no promise of eternal glory beyond the fact of dust; there is a time and a place for these reflections, but sometimes it is healthy to leave these in the background and just reflect on how frail is this solid life of ours, how quickly it passes. Touch your head; feel the eye sockets and know that under this flesh is a skull, symbol of terror and decay; and that skull is you; someday it will throw off the flesh; someday, brainless and vacantly staring, it will be all the face you have left on earth.

Perhaps the pope needs this reminder more than other men. But certainly it is needed by anyone who is placed, however temporarily (and it is always temporary; life is temporary) above his fellow creatures: a parent; a religious superior; a shop foreman, congressman, mayor; the leader of a gang of teen-

joseph mclellan

agers or even the oldest brother in a family. It takes very little to forget that we are dust. And when you ignore the dust, it begins to pile up and it can block your view of reality.

The fact that we are dust is a basic fact of human life. Not the only fact, for we are dust that acts and thinks and feels within it the stirrings of eternity. But dust—limitation, imperfection and a due measure of unhappiness—is the condition of every man, and if we do not remind ourselves of it we will surely be reminded by what happens in our daily lives. So it is good to have the gentle reminder of Ash Wednesday to focus our awareness on our limitations.

But Ash Wednesday is not a feast of despair; it is a feast of humility. If we are indeed dust, we are dust that has been raised by God to a higher status, dust that aspires to union with God. The message of Lent—suffering and confrontation with the facts of sin and death—leads naturally into the message of Easter—joy and resurrection. The two are linked inseparably; without Easter ahead, Ash Wednesday and Lent would be worse than meaningless: morbid. But without Ash Wednesday and the 40 special days that follow it, there would be no need for Easter, no significance to it.

The relation is not merely one of contrast. Lent and Easter are a single reality, existing forever together although we live them one at a time. Without both, our view of the human condition is incomplete. And so, as we kneel on Ash Wednesday and take upon our foreheads the reminder of our mortality, we should look ahead at the same time to Easter and the promise of immortality.

father, forgive them . . . this day thou shalt be with me . . . behold thy son . .

my god, my god . . . I thirst . . . it is finished . . . father, into thy hands . .

the way of the cross today

rev. ronald luka, c.m.f.

preface

Millions of times each year, we Christians follow our Leader around the walls of our churches or through monastery gardens as He trudges His way to Calvary. Saints have written inspiring meditations, artists and sculptors paint and carve graphic presentations, and Christians respond with heartfelt prayers of sorrow and love. It's so easy to recognize Christ and follow the steps He took some 1900 years ago—especially when He's carved in marble or painted in oils.

But do we ever make the Way of the Cross with the Christ who is suffering and dying today? We walk along Christ's path where His blood has been dry for many centuries, but do we ever follow the warm, moist footprints of His blood freshly drawn from the veins of our brothers? Or do we vow with Peter, "I know not the man"?

But how can we miss the Man? He is still being unjustly sentenced, still falling under the Cross, still being stripped of His human dignity, still dying and being buried. How many years must we brush shoulders with Him, kick dust on His bloody footprints, step over His prostrated body, and walk by His Cross as if it were only another billboard? How many times will we have to break bread with Him before we realize that it was with Him that we were walking along the path to Calvary, the road to Emmaus, the streets of our riot-torn cities, and the trails of warworn countries? "Was not our heart burning inside us as He talked to us on the road?"

1
jesus is condemned to death

Look at Christ standing in the courtroom docks throughout the world. He's being tried on trumped-up charges of treason for being about His Father's business in Hungary, Poland, and China. Because He can't raise bond, He's being kept in jail for months on end awaiting trial in Chicago, New York, and Los Angeles. He's being unjustly arraigned before the magistrate in the grocery-store courtroom of some one-horse town. He's being convicted, not for what He did but for what He is, as He stands a few shades darker than His jurors in the courts of racism. Do we know the man? It is He who said, "Whatever you do to these, you do to Me."

"Forgive us for crucifying You a second time in their flesh."
"For we knew not what we did."

2
jesus accepts his cross

Look at Him open His arms to receive the cross of caring for His deformed child. Look at Him accept the cross of old age with its dependence, pain and loneliness. Look at Him cling to the cross of His bed or wheelchair where He is confined for years on end. Look at Him accept the cross of indifference, hostility and hatred. He takes the cross freely and lovingly. At first it is not too heavy. But as the days and years and decades go, its weight becomes heavier. Often we will even hear Him complaining in our neighbor. Yet, instead of helping Him, we avoid Him even more; after all, "That's life!"

"I was sick and you visited Me."
"When did we see You sick and come to You?"
"As long as you did it for one of these you did it for Me"
    (Matt. 25:36f).

jesus falls
the
first time

Look at Him fall under His Cross. He might have fallen into the gutter or slouched into a doorway on skid row. He doesn't look much like God there, but He didn't look like God when He fell into the dirt on Calvary either. In both cases people just stand around and say, "Pick yourself up." Nobody condemns Him because He fell on Calvary. After all, the Cross was heavy, and He was exhausted by the nightlong trial, the scourging and the crowning with thorns. Yet we have only condemnation and disgust for Christ the alcoholic and Christ the dope addict, for Christ the divorcee and Christ the prostitute.

No, He isn't in their sins, just as He isn't in ours. But He is in their persons: They were created in God's image; they are sons of God as Christ is; many of them have become one with Him and us through Baptism, Confirmation and the Eucharist. Can we blame them alone for their fall? Do we know about their trials, scourgings and crownings with thorns? Do we even suspect the part we might have played in knocking them down? Christ had His divine power to pick Himself up on Calvary. These men have exhausted their human power. And what do we do to help them? We complain that they clutter up our streets.

"Why does your Master eat with publicans and sinners?"
"It is not the healthy who need a physician but they who are
sick" (Matt. 9:11f).

4

jesus meets his mother

Look at Him and His mother as they live in the slums of Chicago, Washington, or Rio. Maybe they're on A.D.C. or live on a couple of spoons of beans a day. There might not be any heat or running water; maybe there are rats crawling out of the holes in the walls.

Christ's and Mary's sorrow at this last meeting must have been heavier than the Cross He was carrying. Their sorrow is heavy too in the slums, and they have to live with it day in and day out.

What do we tell them as we relax on our contour chairs? "You're a drain on the taxpayer's dollar." Do we have half the respect for them that we have for the slum lords who might be our suburban neighbors?

After all these years, we still don't get the implications of Christ's searching question, "Who are My mother and My brothers?"

Now what do we think of this Christ? We wish He would show a little more initiative and get out of the slums. We wish some city planner would level all those shacks. It's a pity Christ has ruined the inner city as He has. We hardly dare drive through it now.

"Because he dispensed justice to the weak and the poor, it went well with him."
"Is this not true knowledge of me? says the Lord" (Jer. 22:16).

5

simon helps jesus carry the cross

Look at Simon of Cincinnati turn to get a view of the city as Christ staggers by. "He'll go away in a minute," he tells himself. But He doesn't go away. He stumbles right alongside him.

"Here you go, buddy, help carry this cross!"

"Who me? I didn't do anything. Don't get me involved in this. I have to go to a Rotary meeting at noon and pick the kids up after school. They go to St. Patrick's, you know. I'm Catholic."

"I'm Catholic too," says the soldier. "We wouldn't bother you, but this fellow's going to die before we get Him to the top of the hill to crucify Him. Now pick up that cross, or I'll have to arrest you!"

So Simon picks up the back end of the beam.

"Boy, this thing's heavy. Come on, buddy, let's get moving, I don't have all day. A guy can't even mind his own business. There I was, not bothering anybody, and they saddle me with this. Hope the neighbors don't see me with this guy; I'll never live it down. Simon-do-good they'll call me; always has to stick his neck out. Wish this fellow up front would snap it up. I have a Holy Name meeting tonight; we're planning our spring dance."

"Walk in a manner worthy of the calling with which you were called."

"Bearing with one another in love" (Ephes. 4:1f).

veronica wipes the face of jesus

"Who's this woman coming up here now? Look at that: she broke right through that line of soldiers. Now she's wiping this character's face. Some people just can't mind their own business. She ought to be home cleaning the house. These Apostolic Anns and Busy Bettys, they're everywhere but where they belong. Glad my wife, mother, and sister aren't like that. The kids at home take every minute of their time. We take care of ourselves; everybody else can do the same."

But look at the image Christ imprints on this woman's veil: bloody, sweaty and scarred—but the picture of God Himself. Philip once asked Christ to show him the Father. And Christ told him that those who see Him see the Father. We might be anxious to see Christ, and He assures us that he who sees His handsome or homely features on the faces of his friends and foes, foreigners and family members, neighbors and nomads—sees Him.

"Bear with one another's burdens."
"And so you will fulfill the law of Christ" (Gal. 6:2).

jesus falls the second time

Look, Christ falls again. He has been out in the burning sun all day, picking asparagus, and He just couldn't take the heat and work any longer. He lies there in the dust for a while, before a couple of other migrant workers come to help Him to His feet. He can't work any more today, so He staggers over to the shed He calls home and falls onto a pile of sacks and rags in the corner. It's almost as hot in here as it is out in the fields, but at least He's out of the sun. He hopes His wife and children are okay out in the fields.

He has only been here a few weeks now, and tomorrow He and His family will have to get into the truck with 20 other pickers to head for another state where they'll pick cherries. Year after year He follows the harvest with no place to call home.

Some have tried to organize His fellow pickers, but others won't hear of it. A few people are fighting to help Him, but the others have powerful lobbies. They don't want to pay Him more or provide decent living conditions, because this would lower profits or raise prices.

"Behold the wages of the laborers who reaped your fields,
    which have been kept back by you unjustly."
"Their cry has entered the ear of the Lord of Hosts" (James 5:4).

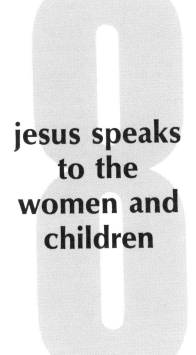

jesus speaks to the women and children

Look at Christ speaking to the women and children. Even amid His own sufferings, He goes out to them as persons, with love and understanding. These are ordinary, common people—like the family next door. While we're seeing Christ in the migrant worker, the imprisoned, the inhabitant of skid row, the soldier on the other side of the world, we can't overlook Him in the people in the room across the hall, the flat downstairs, or the house across the street. He might not always be in extreme need, but He always will need our love, understanding and acceptance.

"Is this not the carpenter's son? Is not His mother called Mary and His brothers James and Joseph?"
"And His sisters, are they not all with us?" (Matt. 13:55f).

jesus falls the third time

Christ gets to His feet, plods on a little, and falls again. And look how He's treated when He's down! As part of a civil rights demonstration, He's only asking that He be treated like a Son of God and share the freedom of His brothers, sons of God too.

How are His requests answered? With police dogs, fire hoses and billy clubs. He's down for the last time now, too weak to fight back. A basic law of human nature is that we help the weak and unprotected. So what happens? We still keep our foot on top of Him, increasing our pressure the more He tries to raise Himself up.

How long will it be before we see the light as Saul did and have the courage to ask and want to know, "Who are You?"

"I am Jesus whom you are persecuting and keeping out of your neighborhoods, unions and schools. I am Jesus whom you force to live in slums, from whom you are running to the suburbs. I am Jesus who said, 'Knock and it will be opened,' and even laws can't make you open your apartments, pools and clubs—and much less your hearts—to Me."

"For in one Spirit we were all baptized into one body."
"Whether Jews or Gentiles, whether slaves or free" (I Cor. 12:13).

jesus is stripped

Look at Him standing on top of the hill, stripped naked. He's running around our cities, poorly fed and housed, too. He's ashamed of His poverty, but what can He do about it? He's poorly educated and His job has been taken by a machine, and He's too old to get another. What else can He do but stand around the corner in His rags? He's ashamed. But who should be more ashamed, He or the society that stripped Him?

He has been in rags for a long time now, but only recently has He become the topic for discussion in plush conference rooms and around luxuriant dinner tables. Even with all this talk and writing about poverty programs, even though a few dollars go into the poor box, even though a few old shirts and shoes are cast His way, how many people ever come by the street corner to encounter Him as a person? If He spoke to us from the crucifix in our parish church, people would flock from all over the country to see the miracle, and in so doing would continue to drive right past Him as He stands stripped on the corner.

"If a brother or a sister be naked and in want of daily food, and one of you say to them: 'Go in peace, be warmed and filled.' "
"Yet you do not give them what is necessary for the body, what does it profit?" (James 2:15f).

27

11
jesus is nailed to the cross

Look at Him as He's nailed to the Cross: as He's locked behind the gates of our mental hospitals, which are so under-staffed that they can do little to help Him and must content themselves with keeping Him out of society; as He's confined to an old people's home because the younger generation can't be bothered with Him; as He's locked in jails and forgotten by the world outside; as He's kept in displaced person camps; as the people of this land of plenty, which says to Him, "Give me your tired, your poor, your huddled masses yearning to be free, the wretched refuse of your teeming shore. Send these, the homeless, tempest-tossed to me," nail Him down with their selfishness and lack of hospitality.

"You shall not molest or oppress an alien, for you were once aliens yourselves in the land of Egypt."
"If you wrong them and they cry out to Me, I will surely hear their cry" (Ex. 22:26).

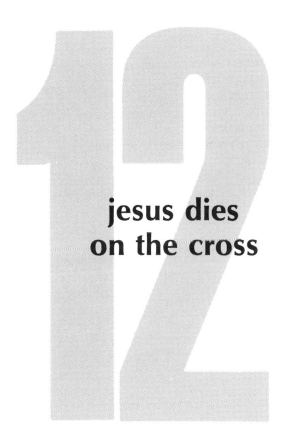

jesus dies on the cross

Look at Him die. Oh, we all must die; nobody gets out of this world alive. But look at Him die prematurely in those deaths that are a continuing witness to man's inhumanity to man. Look at His mangled body getting cut out of that wreck on the highway caused by careless speeding, or drunken driving. Look at Him in the wars, getting cut down like weeds. Look at the preparations we're making to annihilate Him with more and more devastating atomic weapons. Look in your morning newspaper for the times He's murdered each day in gang wars, shootings and stabbings. "As long as you did it to one of these, you did it to Me."

"You have heard that it was said to the ancients, 'You shall not kill.' "
"But I say to you that everyone who is angry with his brother shall be liable to judgment" (Matt. 5:21f).

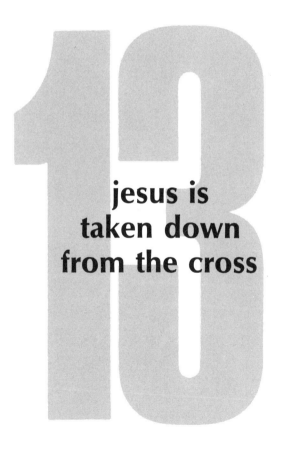

13

jesus is taken down from the cross

The dead body of Christ is taken down from the Cross and placed in the arms of His mother. Look into the hearts of those mothers throughout the world as they find the dead and broken bodies of their children in the bombed-out ruins of what used to be home, as they are awakened in the middle of the night by the police officer with the news that their sons have been killed in a rumble in a slum alley. What sorrow can be compared to their sorrow? And yet we multiply this sorrow by tens, and hundreds, and thousands every week. The tears that flowed on the night of the slaughter of the Innocents in Bethlehem were nothing compared to the deluge of tears that similar useless and brutal slaughters have been wringing from mothers' hearts all these years. When will we ever learn?

"A voice was heard on high of lamentation, of mourning, and weeping, of Rachel weeping for her children."
"And refusing to be comforted for them, because they are not" (Jer. 31:15).

14

the burial of jesus

Then Christ is buried. Unfortunately, this is the most living station for many of us. We don't see Christ as He lives with us, and to the extent that we don't see Him we bury Him. We live with Him in the Mass and other sacraments; we live with Him in our prayers. But we bury Him as He is tried, as He takes His Cross, as He falls, as He is stripped and nailed to the Cross, and as He dies—in our fellowmen. If anything on this Way of the Cross seemed strange to you, or if you caught yourself thinking, "Gee, I never looked at it like that before!" to that extent you've buried Christ—not after He's dead, but alive.

"For as the body is one and has many members, and all the
    members of the body, many as they are, form one body."
"So also it is with Christ" (I Cor. 12:12).

epilogue

1 2 3 4
5 6 7 8
9 10 11 12
13 14 **15**....

the resurrection

Fortunately, we follow a Christ who didn't remain dead and buried. We follow a resurrected and victorious Christ. We often forget this happy ending—the central event in the life of the historical and the mystical Christ. This event will grow in meaningfulness for us, the more we resurrect the buried Christ and serve Him as He walks the way to Calvary today.

a prayer

Let us pray: Christ, our Brother, forgive us for the senseless sorrow we have been causing each other all these years. Let the spirit of Your love take a greater hold on the world that we may begin to experience the joy that only love can give.

Let us realize that everything we do affects You: Every man on the street is You; everyone we read about in the paper is You; everyone with whom we have any contact is You. Help us to love You.

judas

joseph mclellan

The bible tells us relatively little about Judas Iscariot—what kind of person he was and why he performed the betrayal that has made his name synonymous with traitor. He figures prominently in one gospel episode before the final suffering of Jesus. At the time when Mary Magdalene threw herself weeping at the Savior's feet and washed them with precious oils, Judas was the one who complained that the oil could have been sold and the money given to the poor. If we combine this episode with the crucifixion story, we can work up a picture of a man interested in money, a man who probably disapproved of the repentant Magdalene for her lurid past and her outcast status and a man a shade hypocritical, perhaps, who was ready to condemn others before looking with contrition into his own soul.

There is guesswork and some imagination in this picture of Judas, but it holds together. On the other hand, it makes very little allowance for some qualities Judas must have had to make him eligible for the small, original band of apostles. Certainly he didn't fool Jesus into choosing him, and the very fact that he is seldom mentioned in the gospels must mean that, most of the time, he was smoothly integrated into the group, an apostle like the others, not outstanding for good but not for evil either. He was the man who took care of the small treasury of the group and, therefore, surely, one who was well thought of—trusted—by the others. If he had not been a man respected by his colleagues, he would never have had the opportunity to betray the Lord.

The most important piece of evidence for understanding Judas is one that is never mentioned in the gospels simply because it was taken for granted—that he was a man more or less like the rest of us, not a monster of depravity or a maniac, just a good, solid citizen.

Whether he joined the group with a long-range plan of betrayal already in his mind or whether he had a sudden change of heart for unknown reasons is impossible to say. The only explanation given is Luke's statement that Satan entered into him. Whatever the motives may have been, we can probably be sure of one thing: that all the time he was committing the most monstrous betrayal in history, Judas was probably telling himself that he was simply doing his duty as a good citizen, saving the country from a terrible danger, getting rid of an agitator whose ideas could only bring down trouble on everyone.

The full realization of what he had done came later and then, as Matthew tells us, Judas committed suicide. Tracing our way back from that suicide to the moment of betrayal, it does not strain our charity too much to assume that at first Judas was unaware of the full meaning of his act.

It should be easy for us to understand Judas, because each of us in his own life has run into a Judas character, a Judas situation, at one time or another. We have depended on someone, confided, trusted and, when the test came, we have been let down. Not maliciously, not because of hatred or greed, but simply

because people are weak, because they make mistakes, because they are always able to tell themselves that what they are doing is right and necessary—just as Judas surely did.

When a smaller Judas of this kind comes into our own lives, it is good to remember the example of Jesus, who spoke hardly a word of reproach although he knew ahead of time what was to happen. If we find this kind of love hard to imitate, at least we can take it as an inspiration in our own efforts to understand and sympathize with the smaller Judases in our own lives.

We can learn to sympathize because, if we can find traces of Judas in others, we should be able also to find them in ourselves. Judas was the worst, no doubt, but he was not the only apostle who betrayed Jesus. Judas brought the soldiers into Gethsemani, but the other apostles slept there while they should have been sharing the Master's prayer and suffering. The leader of the apostles, Peter, denied three times that he knew Jesus. And all but one of the twelve found it prudent to be somewhere else during the crucifixion.

Betrayal of Jesus Christ, the betrayal that put Judas into history, is a sin to which, in one degree or another, one form or another, no man can plead not guilty. There is no fact of human nature more important to know, none harder to accept.

This realization is so hard, in fact, that we must balance it with another. When we see the face of Judas reflected in our mirror, we must remember that the punishment Judas imposed on himself was far worse than anything called for by the person he betrayed. If Judas did commit an unforgivable sin—and no man can say whether he did or not—it was not the sin of betrayal. It was the sin of despair.

The Christ sees white in Judas's heart
And loves His traitor well;
The God, to angel His new heaven,
Explores His lowest hell.

William Channing Gannett

His enemies planned and plotted how to rid themselves of Jesus of Nazareth. It had to happen, and the sooner the better. "But not during the Passover," they said, "or we'll have a riot on our hands."

This man Jesus and his disciples were quartered in Bethany at the time, in the house of a leper named Simon. That evening while they were eating supper, a woman named Mary came into the room carrying a large jar of perfume. She went over to where Jesus sat and poured the entire jar over him. Several of the disciples became angry and voiced their disapproval. "Why did you do that? What a waste! That perfume was worth a lot of money that could better have been given to the poor."

"Leave her alone," said Jesus. "You may not understand, but really it's a beautiful thing she has just done. You'll always have the poor with you, but I'll not be with you much longer. All she did was to prepare my body for burial a bit ahead of time. Remember this good woman, all of you, and don't forget to tell people about the thoughtful, loving act you have just witnessed."

One of these disciples, the one called Judas Iscariot, knew how anxious and determined the chief priests were to remove Jesus from the scene so he went to them and offered his services. They readily made him part of their

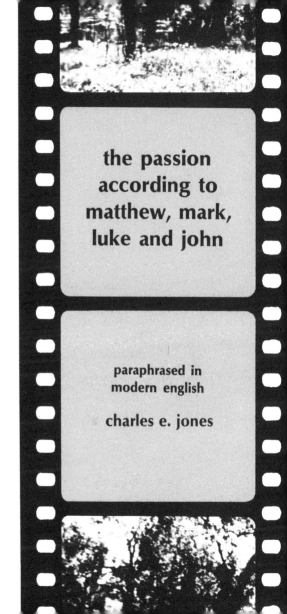

the passion
according to
matthew, mark,
luke and john

paraphrased in
modern english

charles e. jones

conspiracy, and promised a reward of thirty pieces of silver if he could deliver Jesus to them under conditions that would not arouse or upset the people. He agreed to do so when the opportunity next presented itself.

The disciples asked Jesus where they would have their Passover meal. He instructed two of them, Peter and John, to go into the city to a certain place where they would be met by a man carrying a water jar. "Follow him. He will point out a particular house to you. Enter and give the owner this password: 'The teacher has sent us. Where is the room where he and his disciples are to dine tonight?' He'll show you a large upstairs room where you'll find everything we'll need." Peter and John found everything just as Jesus said they would, and they readied the room for the feast.

That evening, Jesus and the twelve entered the upper room for their last meal together. During the meal, Jesus rose from the table, poured some water into a basin and began to wash the disciples' feet, one by one. When he finished, he returned to his place. "Do any of you understand why I have done this?" he asked. "I am your Lord and teacher, and yet, I have just washed your feet. This is an example for you to follow."

A bit later, Jesus interrupted their meal again and startled the group with this statement: "One of you is about to betray me." They were stunned and began to ask, one after the other, "Who, Lord! Surely you don't mean me! Who is it?" "It's one of you twelve," Jesus answered. "One of you who eats at this very table with me tonight will soon betray me. The Son of Man will die as the scriptures say, but, oh how terrible for the man who betrays the Son of Man. It would have been better if he had never been born."

Jesus then took some bread, gave thanks to God, broke it, and passed it around to the disciples, saying, "Take it, this is my body." Next, he raised his cup, gave thanks to God, and passed it to them. "And this is my blood which I will pour out for the forgiveness of mankind's sins. I will not drink wine again until the day I drink the new wine in my Father's kingdom."

Then they sang a hymn together, left the house and went to the Mount of Olives. Jesus said to them: "This very night all of you will run away and desert me." Peter spoke up: "I don't know about the others, Lord, but I'll never leave you." "Remember this," Jesus said to Peter, "before the cock crows tonight, you will deny that you even know me, not once, but three times." Peter answered: "I will never deny knowing you, even if it means I have to die because of it!" And all the others said the same thing.

When they reached the Mount of Olives, Jesus told them to sit and wait while he went off to pray. He took Peter, James and John into the garden with him. "The sorrow I feel is enough to crush me," he said. "Stay here with me and watch." He went on a little further, knelt down and prayed: "Father, if it is possible, please take this cup away from me."

He walked back to Peter, James and John, and found all three of them fast asleep. He woke them and asked: "Why is it that you can't stay awake even for one hour with me?"

He went back and prayed again: "If this cup cannot be taken away, Father, your will be done." He returned to the disciples and found them asleep again.

He left once more. When he returned the third time, he woke them and said: "Come, let us go. The hour has come for the Son of Man to be handed over."

As they were leaving, dozens of torches and lanterns came out of the darkness blocking their way. Armed soldiers and temple guards led the crowd and ringed the little group.

Judas Iscariot stepped out of the crowd, strode up to Jesus and said, "Peace be with you, teacher," and kissed him. That was the prearranged signal. The soldiers came forward and began to tie Jesus' hands. One of the disciples drew his sword and struck out. "Enough," said Jesus, "put your sword away. All who live by the sword will die by the sword." Then addressing himself over the heads of the soldiers to the chief priests and elders who stood hidden well back in the crowd, Jesus said, "Did you have to come with swords and clubs, as if I were a common criminal? I was with you in the temple every day and you did not try to arrest me there. But all this is what the prophets predicted, and you have made it come true."

Then they led him away. All of the chief priests and the entire council gathered for the preliminary hearing, determined to amass enough evidence against Jesus to warrant the death penalty. All sorts of false and flimsy evidence was presented. Stories conflicted. It wasn't going to be easy. Finally, two men testified that they had heard Jesus brag: "I will tear down God's temple and have it built back up again in three days." The high priest stood up and said to Jesus, "What have you got to say about this accusation against you?" But Jesus refused to defend himself. Next the high priest said, "Tell us, are you the Messiah, the son of the living God?" "I am," answered Jesus. At this the high priest tore his robes in mock fury

43

and shouted, "Blasphemy! Send the rest of the witnesses away. We'll not need them now. You just heard him. What do you think? What is your verdict?" They were unanimous against him. "He is guilty and must die!"

Peter had followed the crowd at a safe distance. He slipped in and joined the people huddled around the fire in the outside courtyard. A woman recognized him and said, "This man was with him! You're a friend of Jesus, aren't you?" But Peter denied it, loudly, for all to hear: "I don't know what you're talking about, woman, I don't even know the man." Another spotted him and exclaimed to the crowd, "He is one of them! He was with Jesus of Nazareth!" Again Peter denied it, answering, "I am not. I swear that I don't even know the man!" A little while later, one of the bystanders accused Peter again: "You can't deny that you're one of them. Even the way you speak gives you away. You're from Galilee, aren't you?" Then Peter vowed again: "May God punish me if I'm not telling the truth! I don't know that man!" Just then a cock crowed. Peter recalled what Jesus had said earlier that evening. He fled from the courtyard, went off by himself and wept bitterly.

The soldiers who guarded Jesus through the night mocked and beat him. They blindfolded him, slapped his face and said: "Prophesy for us, Messiah! Tell us which one of us it was who just hit you."

When Judas Iscariot heard that Jesus had been condemned, he repented and returned to the chief priests with his reward in hand. "I have betrayed an innocent man," he said. "Don't bother us," they answered, "that's your problem." He threw the money down and left. Shortly after, his body was found hanging from a tree.

Early the next morning they put Jesus in chains and led him off to the palace of the Roman governor.

The Jews could not enter the governor's palace with their prisoner because they had to keep themselves ritually clean for the Passover meal. So Pilate came out into the yard to meet them. "Why do you bring this man before me?" he asked. "What has he done?" They accused him of many things, of misleading the people, of telling them not to pay taxes to the Emperor, and of claiming to be Christ, the King of the Jews.

Pilate said to them, "Why don't you try him according to your own law?" "Because," they replied, "we're not allowed to put anyone to death. You know that, it's Roman law."

Pilate turned to Jesus, "Are you the King of the Jews?" he asked. "You say it," answered Jesus, "I am a king." Then Pilate spoke to the assembled crowd again, "I have no reason to condemn this man." But they kept insisting and

shouting their accusations, "He is causing riots among our people. He started his troublemaking in Galilee and now he has come here to arouse the people with more lies."

When Pilate heard that Jesus was a Galilean, he seized upon the chance to rid himself of the responsibility. He declared that Jesus should first have a hearing with Herod who was ruler of the region of Galilee.

Herod was in Jerusalem at the time, and welcomed the opportunity to see this man he had been hearing so much about. He hoped that perhaps he might even see him perform a miracle. Herod asked Jesus many questions, but Jesus would not answer. So Herod sent him back to Pilate.

Pilate called the chief priests and other leaders together and said to them: "You have brought this man before me. I have questioned him in your presence about all the things you accuse him of, but I find no guilt. Nor did Herod find him guilty. The man has done nothing, as far as I can see, to deserve the death sentence. I will have him whipped and set free."

Then Pilate, hoping they would take pity, brought Jesus out again and said, "Look at the man!" But this infuriated

the crowd all the more and they shouted over and over: "Crucify him! Crucify him!"

Pilate then said, "According to custom I must set a prisoner free during the Passover. This man who claims to be King of the Jews, shall I set him free for you?" "No, no," they chanted, "not him. We want Barabbas. Set Barabbas free."

Pilate asked once more. "Why shouldn't I free him? What crime has he committed?" But they just kept shouting at the top of their voices, "Crucify him, nail him to the cross, crucify him!"

Pilate saw that it was no use, that a riot might break out, so he took a bowl of water, washed his hands in front of the crowd, and said: "I am not responsible for the death of this man! You are!"

Then the soldiers took Jesus inside the Governor's palace. They stripped off his clothes, put a purple robe over his shoulders, made a crown of thorns and put it upon his head. They spat on him, hit him with sticks and knelt before him, taunting, "Long live the King of the Jews."

When they tired of their games, they took off the robe, put the cross upon his shoulders and led him out to be crucified.

Along the way the soldiers seized a man named Simon and forced him to help with the cross because its weight was now more than Jesus could bear.

A large crowd followed the grim procession. People poured out into the streets to watch. Many women were weeping and wailing for him. Jesus stopped and said to them: "Women of Jerusalem, do not weep for me, but for yourselves and for your children."

Finally, they came to the place of execution, Golgotha, which means "the place of the skull." They offered him wine mixed with a drug, but Jesus would not drink it.

They nailed him to the cross, and lifted it into place. The soldiers divided his clothes among them by throwing dice, and above his head they placed a sign which read, "This is Jesus, the King of the Jews." Then they crucified two thieves, one on each side of Jesus.

The people stood about and threw insults at Jesus: "So you can tear the temple down and rebuild it in three days! Now let's see you come down from the cross and save yourself!" The soldiers made fun of him too, saying: "Let us see the Messiah, the King of the Jews, come down from the cross."

"Forgive them, Father!" said Jesus, "They don't know what they're doing."

One of the thieves joined in: "If you're the Messiah, save yourself and us!" But the other thief rebuked the first one, saying, "We deserve our fate, but this man is innocent. He has done nothing wrong. Leave him alone." Jesus said to him, "This very day you will be in paradise with me."

When Jesus saw his mother standing at the foot of the cross with his beloved disciple, John, he said to her, "Woman, there is your son," and to John he said, "There is your mother."

The sky had been covered with darkness for three hours. At three o'clock in the afternoon, Jesus cried out, "My God, my God, why have you abandoned me?" Some of the people heard him and said, "Listen, he is calling for Elijah. Let's see if Elijah comes to help him."

One of them soaked a sponge in wine and offered it up to him, but he wouldn't take it.

"It is finished," he said. Then he bowed his head and died.

and we will follow after

Sickness, pain, and death are among the great realities of human life. They are also among life's great mysteries. They remind us always of the very fragile nature of our existence on earth, and of the delicate balance of life in the world.

We look upon them with questions in our hearts because the sight of them always poses problems for us. The experience of pain, sickness, and death are a shock to us. Man was meant for better things. The desires of our life are ideals so far above them that we are shaken by contact with them. Somehow we would have them pass us by forever.

For those who have been seriously sick, for those who have suffered poignant pain of body, and as a consequence, experienced some firsthand projections of their own death, the reality of a better world as outlined in the Apocalypse is a sweet one: "And God will wipe away every tear from their eyes, and death shall be no more; neither shall there be mourning, nor crying, nor pain any more, for the former things have passed away."

Though "the former things" shall not pass us by, as we would prefer, there will come a most glorious time when they shall pass away. It is made plain once more that the greatest and wildest yearnings of our hearts are, after all,

follow
follow
follow
follow
follow
follow
follow
follow
follow
follow
follow
follow
follow
follow
follow
follow
follow
follow

due to be fulfilled. Sickness, pain, and death are passing events to something better.

The basic desire in the heart of man to be whole when he has been injured, to be sound in mind and body again when he is sick, is a desire befitting human nature. Or, if it is not possible to be well then the desire to be able to bear suffering patiently as becomes a man, or, when there is danger of death to have some hope against it by being able, in the last extremity, to call upon the name of the Lord in the inevitable aloneness—these are human things that bring us close to Christ in his passion.

It is not a blessing to be sick. The blessing of the sick man is, in the resemblance of Christ, accepting and redeeming the world with his pain and suffering. For, Christ too was strong and his strength was reduced to nothing; he too was doing a good work which was interrupted; his good and useful life was likewise brought to an end in the mystery of death.

But something new happened with Christ. In Christ all these sad things are brought into a new and joyful dimension. Christ heals permanently and finally makes immortal our being; Christ fulfills man's desire for wholeness, for soundness, for immortality. He rose. He is the firstborn from the dead. And we will follow after.

eugene s. geissler

emember ma
an rememb
er man rem
nember man
n remember
r man remer
ember man r
remember r
man remem
nber man re
emember ma
an rememb
er man rem
nember man
n remember
r man remer
ember man

**their
lent
is
over
and
their
easter
won**

william crosswell doane

I'm sorry

"I'm sorry."

Simple words—but are there any words in the language more difficult for us to say? They strike right to the heart of what gives our life its flavor, the feeling of our own value and importance. They require us to examine ourselves, to judge ourselves by a hard standard and to cut off, to repudiate what we have done or said; to commit radical surgery on what we *are*.

It is easier, when we are wrong, to bristle and defend ourselves, to resist any effort at correction from ourselves or—much more so—from others. It is partly a question of momentum; when you are moving in a certain direction, it is much easier to keep going than to stop or to turn. But even more, it is a matter of identity; I am, in a sense, what I have done and anything that criticizes or reverses my actions is an attack on me.

When we talk about "self-denial," we usually mean the decision to deprive ourselves of something that we like. It is done, like an athlete's exercises, to strengthen our self-control; we practice on little things so that we will be ready when a big challenge comes.

But there is another meaning for self-denial—a meaning which corresponds exactly to what the words say—renunciation of ourselves, of the wrongs we

have done and have thus made a part of us. This is also the true meaning of penance: self-examination, admission of wrong and the decision to change. For most people, it is the hardest thing in the world.

And that is as good a reason as any for the existence of Lent. A thing that is hard to do alone and on your own initiative becomes easier when you are joined by others and are engaging in an action with a tradition that has been built up through the centuries.

The danger, of course, in mass participation and in the use of an ageless ritual, is that it may become too easy. You can let the experience slide by without really living it. If you say the proper prayers because you have been told that is the thing to do, the chances are that you are not really praying. If you observe Lent because everyone in your family does, you are not really observing Lent. You are going through the motions.

There are ways to avoid this danger. If you are merely aware of it, that is already half the battle. And if you keep in mind that it probably isn't doing any good unless it is difficult—unless it hurts—that may be the other half.

The important thing is to keep in mind what you are really saying as you go through the various Lenten practices:

"I'm sorry."

joseph mclellan

ONE WAY

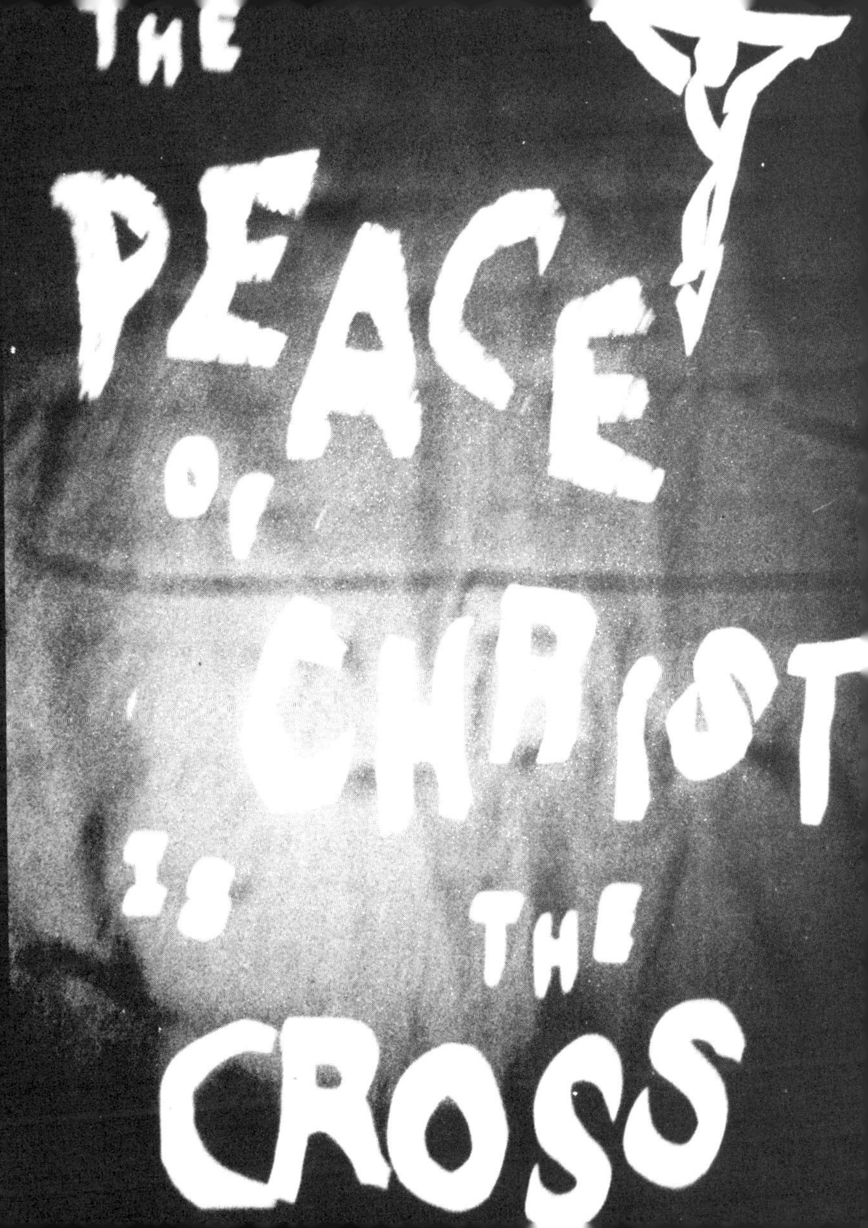

lenten prayers

dolores boyle

I shall change; you'll see.
I promise to be different
   tomorrow.
But what I fail to see
   each day
Is: tomorrow becomes today
   in the most uncanny way.

Lord, You know me through
   and through.
Please, do me a favor.
Pinch my tongue so I
   won't be unkind to my
   brothers
Rap my knuckles, if I
   strike out in anger.
Mow down the thoughts
I'd rather not have
Please, make me perfect
   for you —
By Easter.

the way of the cross today for children

charles e. jones

1 jesus is condemned to death

Look at these boys jeering and shaking their fists in anger at a negro family moving into their neighborhood. You can see the bitterness reflected in their young faces. You can almost hear the mob chanting "Crucify Him!"

What a pitiful scene! How terribly sad that they don't realize what they are doing. In condemning others because of their race, color or religion, we condemn Jesus to death all over again.

How alone you must have felt, dear Jesus, when the crowd mocked you and shouted "Crucify Him!" Forgive us as you forgave them, and teach us to love and accept one another.

jesus accepts his cross

2

Dragging himself along on his crutches, this crippled boy moves slowly down the hospital corridor. As he gets closer to the sunlight outside, he hears the sound of children running and playing. His cross grows heavy.

For most of us, our crosses are nothing more than little trials. Do we make them heavier by complaining, or do we accept them and keep going like Jesus and this brave little boy?

Dear Jesus, you carried the heaviest cross of all. Give us the courage to accept our cross as you accepted yours. We know that you will be there beside us.

3 jesus falls the first time

This little girl writing on the blackboard looks like any other little girl in your school. She isn't though. She's retarded. A simple circle that you were able to draw even before you started school is a big struggle for her.

Little things that come easy for us are terribly hard for children like her. They carry a heavy cross. Like Jesus on the way to Calvary, they fall many times.

How painfully heavy your cross must have been, my Jesus. Stay close to all your children who stumble under the burden of their crosses. We cannot go on without you.

jesus meets his mother

4

"Please don't cry, Mother!"

A frightened Vietnamese boy, dressed in rags, looks up into his mother's tear-filled eyes. He doesn't know what's wrong. He only knows he doesn't want to see his mother cry.

When Jesus and His mother, Mary, met on the road to Calvary, their hearts were filled with sorrow. Their sorrow is shared today by the mothers and sons of all the wartorn nations of the world.

My loving Jesus, it must have hurt you deeply to see your mother weeping so pitifully for you, her only son. Help us always to be a comfort to our own mothers as you were to Mary.

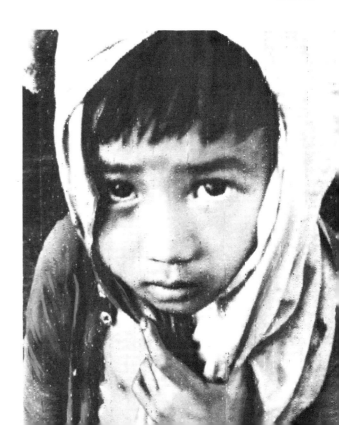

5   simon helps jesus carry his cross

"Where are you from, little boy?"

"From Texas, New Jersey, Indiana, wherever there are crops to pick. My father and mother work in the fields all day, and I bring them water. I'd like to go to school every day the way you do, and have a bicycle of my own to ride—but I'm the son of a migrant worker."

Simon didn't choose to help Jesus with the cross. The soldiers made him. But this little boy takes up his cross willingly. He loves his parents and wants to help them.

No one wanted to help you, Jesus, when you weakened under the weight of your cross. We will always be willing to help others because we love you.

veronica wipes the face of jesus

6

The children of Africa learn to live with pain. This little boy suffers from an eye infection. His mother carefully applies the medicine that has just reached their village. It soothes, and he is very grateful, even though he knows it will be a long time before more medicine arrives.

Jesus showed His gratitude to Veronica by leaving the likeness of His sacred face on her veil. Someday a smile may light this little boy's face to thank those who have helped him.

Jesus, you turned to reward Veronica, even though you had scarcely the strength to move. We turn to you with all our love, ever grateful for the suffering you endured to save us.

7 jesus falls the second time

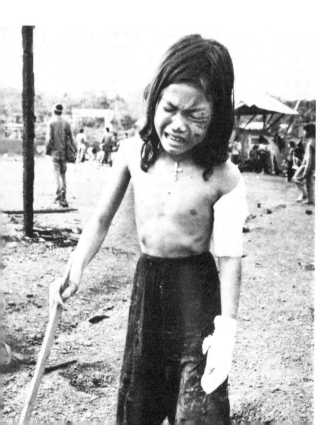

The cross of war is always heaviest for the innocent children. A little girl limps along a dusty road in Vietnam. Her village has been destroyed, she is alone and frightened. The pain of her wounds is more than she can bear. She begins to cry.

Jesus was innocent too, but every time He fell the soldiers lifted the heavy cross back onto His bleeding shoulders. And today the tears of the children of war weigh Him down again.

The brutal cross crushed you to the ground, dear Jesus, but you rose again and struggled on. The children of war cannot bear their heavy crosses alone. Please give them your strength.

jesus speaks to the women and children 8

Leave your comfortable home. Take a trip in the family car. Go deep into the Appalachians, through the shanty towns of the deep south, past the Indian reservations of the west, or just through the slums of your own city. There they wait—in two-room shacks without windows or doors—poverty-stricken families without hope.

Jesus stopped on His sorrowful journey to speak to the weeping women and children of Jerusalem. This despairing mother and her hungry children wait at their door for us today. How long must they suffer?

Dear Jesus, even in your agony you were moved by the sorrow and suffering of others. Help us to see the needs of those around us. Teach us to be more generous to those who need our help.

9 jesus falls the third time

Just an hour ago this little Turkish girl ran happily down the mountainside with her friends. Then, in an instant, a terrible earthquake destroyed the entire village. She has searched the ruins in vain for her family. Tearfully, she sinks to her knees in the rubble and weeps.

Once again Jesus lifted Himself up under the heavy cross and continued on His torturous journey. This little girl shares His suffering today as she struggles down the mountainside with her own cruel cross.

How very much you must love us, dear Jesus, to have been so willing a victim to so much pain. We offer all our crosses in return, to show our love and devotion to you.

jesus is stripped of his garments 10

No one laughs, as children usually do. Not in this refugee camp. These sad-eyed youngsters fetch their daily water ration in tin cans. They fled from their homes as the battle drew near. Everything they owned is gone—all but the tattered clothes on their backs. What will they do now?

When Jesus, the hope of the world, reached the place of His crucifixion, the soldiers ripped His garments from His bleeding back. These children have been stripped of hope for the future by a brutal war.

They stripped away your garments, my loving Jesus, but they could not take away your undying love for all of us. Help us to keep our hearts free to love you above all things.

11 jesus is crucified

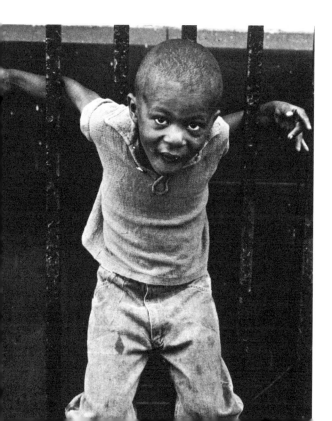

Hang from your cross, little boy. It's only a game—or is it? It's hard to pretend that the thorns of prejudice and the nails of poverty don't hurt. It's hard to pretend that you don't hear those people who say that the color of your skin makes you different.

Jesus, our brother, suffered and died on the cross because He loved all mankind, the people of every nation, of every shade and color. This little boy is Jesus' brother and our brother too. We must love him. If we don't, we crucify Jesus all over again.

They were afraid of you, dear Jesus, because you too were different, and so they crucified you. Bring us closer to all our brothers so that we may learn to love them.

jesus dies on the cross

She tries hard not to remember, but how can this little Korean war orphan ever forget? Her entire family, her mother and father, her sisters and brothers, all of them are dead. She tries hard but she can't help remembering. A tear falls from her eye.

Jesus loved us so much that He died on the cross for us. He did not leave us though. He is with us always, and will comfort us in our loneliness and despair.

Jesus, my redeemer, you suffered and died on the cross to save us. Our love for you will never die. We give ourselves to you; do with us what you will.

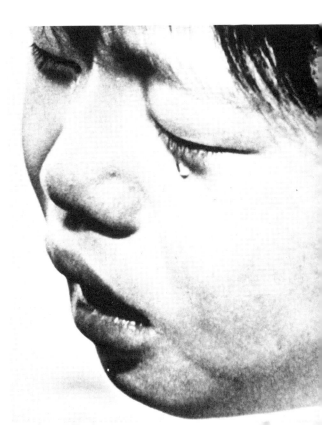

13 jesus is taken down from the cross

It's Friday afternoon. The children laugh gaily on the way home from school. Suddenly, a truck skids on the wet pavement and crashes into the side of their bus. The rescue workers remove a little boy from the twisted wreckage.

When the ordeal was over for Jesus, His lifeless body was placed in the arms of His grief-stricken mother. This little boy will suffer no more. His tragic death is the cross that all who loved him must now carry.

Your sacrifice is finished, my Jesus. You have given your life in obedience to the will of your father. We too accept whatever our heavenly father asks of us.

jesus is laid in the tomb

14

A tear can be seen on the cheek of the little stone angel standing its silent vigil over the grave of a little child. The world is dotted with the crosses of the innocent victims of disease, hunger, poverty, tragic accidents and senseless wars.

A huge stone sealed the tomb where Jesus lay, and the soldiers took up their watch in the quiet darkness. Today, sounds of weeping break the stillness near the graves of once laughing children.

The tomb is sealed, dear Jesus, but the doors of your father's house are now open to us all. Stay with us so that we do not lose the way.

meditation

barry lopez

He told the twelve he would meet them
later in the city, that he wished to be
alone now. They understood and departed . . .

. . . and he went into the woods to pray.

It was still. Like death in the afternoon. He sat back against the rough bark of an old oak and the pain and loneliness went out of him for a moment. He closed his eyes and lay his head to rest on his knees and fell deep into his own mind.

Sunlight filtered. Trees grew imperceptibly. Flowers waved barely.

He searched in his mind briefly for the thoughts he'd been with a moment before but they were gone. Black thoughts, of the darkness ahead.

Golgotha. It flashed across him again like a hot knife in an alley. He could not shut it out. It haunted him and he was heavy with darkness.

He reached out to his side and his fingers drifted slowly over the gnarled bark. Gnarled like Joseph's hands. Callused. His own hands were callused too. It was a good thing to work with your hands he thought, to work with wood. He remembered Joseph teaching him to use the adze to sheer off a strip of wood so thin you could almost see through it. He wondered if Joseph had ever made a cross.

The calluses on his hands were the badge of

his trade, a shield, like the tree's bark, against the small dangers of life; but it was the calluses on his feet that he now pondered. Were those the marks of a madman, he wondered. He closed his eyes again and he could see the dusty roads, the rough brick and the cobble and the gravel chewing at his sandals, and then at his feet. How many miles had he wandered. How many had laughed and spat in his face. He opened his eyes again and was aware of the trees. They never went anywhere.

They were so full of death. They were so full of life. Silent. Wise, he thought. Trees are wise, and they have the serenity that comes with wisdom.

How often he'd sought their shadows. He'd clung to them in dark hours, resting his throbbing head against their cool bark, waiting for the pain to abate. It was as though the tree could suck the fire from his mind. He would cry sometimes in frustration and confusion, feel his calluses scraping the ridged bark, and leave tears to dry on leaves. His soul rumbled day and night in frustration and despair. A thousand times he came close to forsaking it all, renouncing it all, disappearing into the

desert, emerging in a new place, a place where he was not known. But he would come back to the trees, wind among them like a vine, and find peace and incredible strength. It was cool in their shade. It was easy to walk among them and forget.

He couldn't forget.

It haunted him. He could see the nails driving through his hands, the cross stretched across the sky, his broken body slung from it like a broken branch.

He wondered what they would do with the cross. Drag it off? Firewood for some stranger's meal? Would the twelve gain possession of it (would they even come out and be seen in the street), hide it somewhere in a dark cellar, buried under casks of red wine and wheels of goat cheese.

He felt empty. Tired. Drained. He looked up along the trunk of the knotted tree he sat against, up through its branches to the sky. Leaves quaking in the light. Little hands.

He heard a bird's shrill twitter and turned to see another veer off and disappear into the leaves. How many birds sat hidden, silent in the shadows.

How many nests in limbs' crooks, how many squirrels, how many beetles lay asleep beneath the bark. What of worms and rabbits tucked in among the roots.

His eye jumped from limb to leaf to trunk to leaf and fell dead on a healed scar. There was another above it. And another. Steps. Above them on a thick forked branch lay a single rotting board. And people, too, he thought. The trees harbor people, and children know enough to build tree houses.

He heard a bell in the distance. The sun was falling. They were bringing the flocks in. He could not stay longer, he reminded himself, rising to his feet. They would worry.

He felt so alone. Off in the distance he could see lonely trees against the afternoon sky. He shut his eyes slowly and saw the winter shore, the bleakness, the loneliness, the failing light. His mind cut through the future like a knife and he saw more winter shores. But he drew hope from them. He had no choice. He'd had enough of pain.

Cedar he suddenly thought. That's what they would use for the cross.

everyman's
way of the cross

clarence enzler

Introduction

Christat
speaks
These fourteen steps
that you are now about to walk
you do not take alone.

I walk with you.

Though you are you,
and I am I,
yet we are truly one—
one Christ

And therefore
My way of the cross
two thousand years ago
and your "way" now
are also one.

But note this difference.
My life was incomplete until I crowned it
by My death.
Your fourteen steps
will only be complete
when you have crowned them
by your life.

1 Jesus Is Condemned

Christ speaks

In Pilate's hands, My other self,
I see My Father's will.
Though Pilate is unjust,
he is the lawful governor
and he has power over Me.

And so the Son of God obeys a son of man.

If I can bow to Pilate's rule
because this is My Father's will,
can you refuse obedience
to those whom I place over you?

Man replies

My Jesus, Lord,
obedience cost You Your life.
For me it costs an act of will—
no more—
and yet how hard it is for me to bend.

Remove the blinders from my eyes
that I may see that it is You whom I obey
in all who govern me.

Lord, it is You.

2 Jesus Takes His Cross

Christ

This cross, this chunk of tree,
is what My Father chose for Me.

The crosses you must bear
are largely products of your daily life.
And yet My Father chose them, too,
for you.

Receive them from His hands.

Take heart, My other self,
I will not let your burdens grow
one ounce too heavy for your strength.

Man

My Jesus, Lord, I take my daily cross.
I welcome the monotony
that often marks my day,
discomforts of all kinds,
the summer's heat, the winter's cold,
my disappointments, tensions, setbacks, cares.

Remind me often that
In carrying my cross,
I carry Yours with You.
And though I bear a sliver only
of Your cross,
You carry all of mine, except a sliver,
in return.

3 Jesus Falls

Christ
The God who made the universe,
and holds it in existence by His will alone,
becomes, as man, too weak to bear
a piece of timber's weight.

How human in His weakness is the Son of Man.

My Father willed it thus.
I could not be your model otherwise.

If you would be My other self,
you also must accept without complaint
your human frailties.

Man
Lord Jesus, how can I refuse?

I willingly accept my weaknesses,
my irritations and my moods,
my headaches and fatigue,
all my defects of body, mind, and soul.

Because they are Your will for me,
these "handicaps," of my humanity,
I gladly suffer them.

Make me content with all my discontents,
but give me strength to struggle after You.

4 Jesus Meets His Mother

Christ
My Mother sees Me whipped.
She sees Me kicked and driven like a beast.
She counts My every wound.
But though her soul cries out in agony,
no protest or complaint escapes her lips
or even enters on her thoughts

She shares My martyrdom—
and I share hers.
We hide no pain, no sorrow,
from each other's eyes.
This is My Father's will.

Man
My Jesus, Lord,
I know what You are telling me.
To watch the pain of those we love
is harder than to bear our own.

To carry my cross after You,
I, too, must stand and watch
the sufferings of my dear ones;
the heartaches, sicknesses and grief
of those I love.

And I must let them watch mine, too.

I do believe—for those who love You
all things work together unto good.
They must!

5 Simon Helps Jesus

Christ
My strength is gone;
I can no longer bear the cross alone.
And so the legionnaires
make Simon give Me aid.

This Simon is like you, My other self.

Give Me your strength.

Each time you lift some burden from
another's back,
you lift as with your very hand
the cross's awful weight
that crushes Me.

Man
Lord, make me realize
that every time I wipe a dish,
pick up an object off the floor,
assist a child in some small task,
or give another preference
in traffic or the store;
each time I feed the hungry,
clothe the naked,
teach the ignorant,
or lend my hand in any way—
it matters not to whom—
my name is Simon.
And the kindness I extend to them
I really give to You.

6 Veronica Helps Jesus

Christ
Can you be brave enough, My other self,
to wipe My bloody face?

Where is My face, you ask?

At home whenever eyes fill up with tears,
at work when tensions rise,
on playgrounds,
in the slums,
the courts, the hospitals, the jails—
wherever suffering exists—
My face is there.
And there I look for you
to wipe away My blood and tears.

Man
Lord, what You ask is hard.
It calls for courage and self-sacrifice,
and I am weak.
Please, give me strength.
Don't let me run away because of fear.

Lord, live in me and act in me
and love in me.
And not in me alone—in all men—
so that we may reveal
no more Your bloody but Your glorious face
on earth.

7 Jesus Falls Again

Christ This seventh step, My other self,
is one that tests your will.
From this fall learn to persevere
in doing good.

The time will come
when all your efforts seem to fail
and you will think, "I can't go on."

The˒ turn to Me,
My heavy-laden one,
and I will give you rest.

Trust Me and carry on.

Man Give me your courage, Lord.
When failure presses heavily on me
and I am desolate,
stretch out Your hand
to lift me up.

I know I must not cease,
but persevere, in doing good.

But help me, Lord.
Alone there's nothing I can do.
With You, I can do anything You ask.
I will.

8 Jesus Consoles the Women

Christ How often had I longed to take
the children of Jerusalem
and gather them to Me. But they refused.

But now these women weep for Me
and My heart mourns for them—
mourns for their sorrows that will come.

I comfort those who seek to solace Me.

How gentle can you be, My other self,
How kind?

Man My Jesus,
Your compassion
in Your passion
is beyond compare.

Lord, teach me, help me learn.
When I would snap at those
who hurt me with their ridicule,
those who misunderstand,
or hinder me with some misguided helpfulness,
those who intrude upon my privacy—
then help me curb my tongue.

May gentleness become my cloak.

Lord, make me kind like You.

9 The Third Fall

Christ
Completely drained of strength
I lie, collapsed, upon the cobblestones.
My body cannot move.
No blows, no kicks, can rouse it up.

And yet My will is Mine.

And so is yours.

Know this, my other self,
your body may be broken,
but no force on earth
and none in hell can take away your will.

Your will is yours.

Man
My Lord, I see You take a moment's rest
then rise and stagger on.
So I can do because my will is mine.

When all my strength is gone
and guilt and self-reproach
press me to earth and seem to hold me fast,
protect me from the sin of Judas—
save me from despair!

Lord, never let me feel that any sin of mine
is greater than Your love.
No matter what my past has been
I can begin anew.

10 Jesus Is Stripped

Christ
Behold, my other self,
the poorest King who ever lived.
Before My creatures I stand stripped.
The cross—my deathbed—
even this is not My own.

Yet who has ever been so rich?

Possessing nothing, I own all—
My Father's love.

If you, too, would own everything,
be not solicitous
about your food, your clothes, your life.

Man
My Lord, I offer you my all—
whatever I possess, and more, my self.

Detach me from the craving for prestige,
position, wealth.
Root out of me
all trace of envy of my neighbor
who has more than I.
Release me from the vice of pride,
my longing to exalt myself,
and lead me to the lowest place.

May I be poor in spirit, Lord,
so that I can be rich in You.

11 Jesus Is Crucified

Christ Can you imagine what a crucifixion is?

My executioners stretch My arms;
they hold My hand and wrist against the wood
and press the nail until it stabs My flesh.
Then with one heavy hammer smash
they drive it through—
and pain
bursts like a bomb of fire in My brain.

They seize the other arm;
and agony again explodes.

Then raising up My knees
so that My feet are flat against the wood,
they hammer them fast, too.

Man My God,
I look at You and think:
Is my soul worth this much?

What can I give You in return?

I here and now accept for all my life
whatever sickness, torment, agony may come.
To every cross I touch my lips.

O blessed cross that lets me be—
with You—
a co-redeemer of my fellowmen.

12 Jesus Dies

Christ The cross becomes a pulpit now—
"Forgive them, Father . . .
You will be with Me in Paradise . . .
There is your mother . . . There . . . your son . . .
I thirst . . .
It is complete."

To speak I have to raise Myself
by pressing on My wrists and feet,
and every move engulfs Me in new waves of agony.

And then, when I have borne enough,
have emptied My humanity,
I let My mortal life depart.

Man My Jesus, God,
what can I say or do?

I offer *my* death with all its pains,
accepting now
the time and kind of death in store for me.
Not by a single instant
would I lengthen my life's span.

I offer You my death for my own sins
and those of all my fellowmen.

My God! My God! Forsake us not.
We know not what we do.

13 Jesus Is Taken Down

Christ   The sacrifice is done.
Yes, My Mass is complete;
but not My mother's
and not yours, My other self.

My mother still must cradle in her arms
the lifeless body of the Son she bore.

You, too, must part from those you love,
and grief will come to you.

In your bereavements think of this:
A multitude of souls were saved
by Mary's sharing in My Calvary.
Your grief can also be the price of souls.

Man   I beg You, Lord,
help me accept the partings that must come—
from friends who go away,
my children leaving home,
and most of all, my dear ones
when You shall call them to Yourself.

Then, give me grace to say:
"As it has pleased You, Lord,
to take them home,
I bow to Your most holy will
And if by just one word
I might restore their lives
against Your will, I would not speak."
Grant them eternal joy.

14 Jesus Is Buried

Christ   So ends My mortal life.

But now another life begins for Mary,
and for Magdalen,
for Peter and for John, and you.

My work as man is done.
My work within and through My Church
must now commence.

I look to you, My other self.

Day in, day out, from this time forth,
be My apostle—victim—saint.

Man   My Jesus, Lord,
You know my spirit is as willing
as my flesh is weak.

The teaching You could not impart,
the sufferings You could not bear,
the works of love You could not do
in Your short life on earth,
let me impart, and bear, and do
through You.

But I am nothing, Lord.
Help me!

Conclusion

Christ   I told you at the start, My other self,
My life was not complete
until I crowned it by My death.
Your "way" is not complete
unless you crown it by your life.

Accept each moment as it comes to you,
with faith and trust
that all that happens has My mark on it.
A simple *fiat,* this is all it takes;
a breathing in your heart,
"I will it, Lord."

So seek Me not in far-off places.
I am close at hand.
Your workbench, office, kitchen,
these are altars
where you offer love.
And I am with you there.

Go now! Take up your cross
and with your life
complete your way.

in death
there is life

The epilogue of life is death
and man enters death at the end of life—
except that sometimes death
overtakes him
while yet a child just beginning
or a youth on the rise
or a man in the middle of his powers . . .

For all the end of the body as we know it
is a cemetery—
a plot of earth
no bigger than a man can encompass
falling exhausted to the ground.

And for a while
a marker marks the spot.

But the unfinished man goes on.
His spirit lives.
This we must believe.
Otherwise life is absurd
impossible
a contradiction of man's endless
search for endless meaning.

His unfinished spirit goes on
not only in those who come after him
who were born of him
but he himself goes on—
his own particular self
the self that he has made
unique, irreplaceable piece of being—
goes on to better things . . .
which no eye has seen nor ear has heard . . .

When that happens to a man
then he knows
that death is a friend
that death is a beginning
that in death there is life.

eugene s. geissler

89

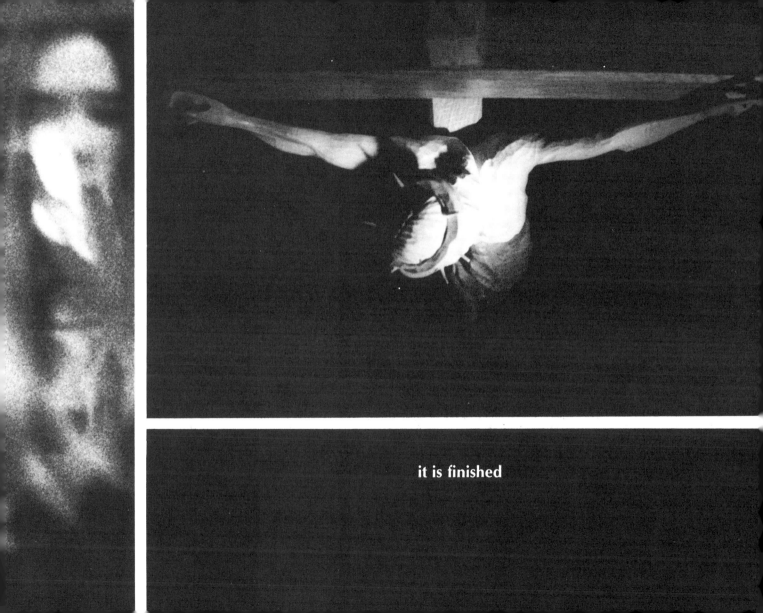

it is finished

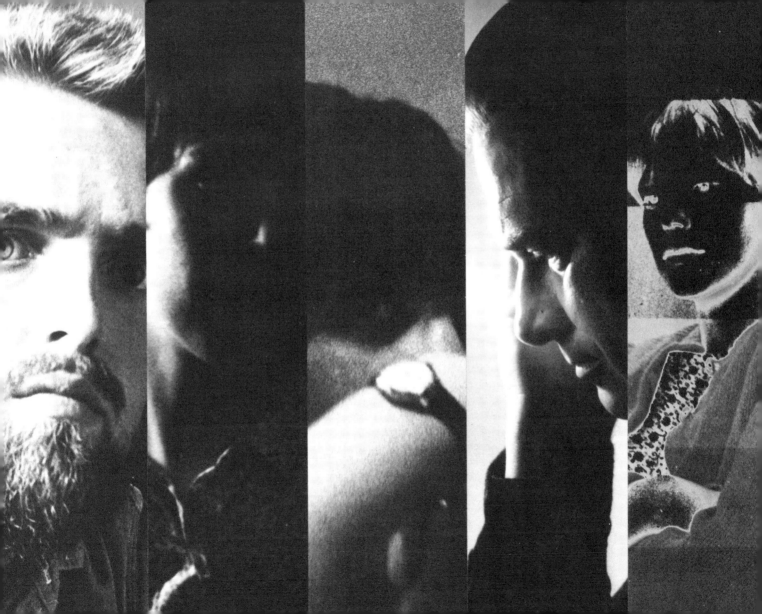

remember man

remember

......we've got a good thing going now!